STATE PROFILES

NEVADA

BY COLLEEN SEXTON

BLASTOFF!
DISCOVERY

BELLWETHER MEDIA • MINNEAPOLIS, MN

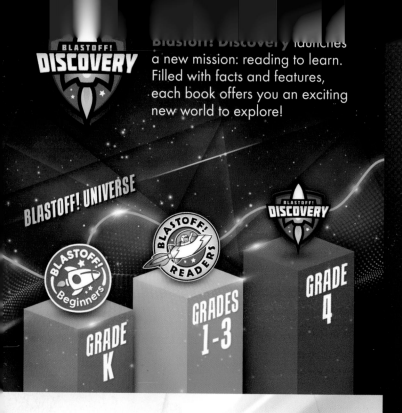

Blastoff! Discovery launches a new mission: reading to learn. Filled with facts and features, each book offers you an exciting new world to explore!

BLASTOFF! UNIVERSE

BLASTOFF! Beginners — GRADE K

BLASTOFF! READERS — GRADES 1-3

DISCOVERY — GRADE 4

This edition first published in 2022 by Bellwether Media, Inc.

No part of this publication may be reproduced in whole or in part without written permission of the publisher.
For information regarding permission, write to Bellwether Media, Inc., Attention: Permissions Department,
6012 Blue Circle Drive, Minnetonka, MN 55343.

Library of Congress Cataloging-in-Publication Data

Names: Sexton, Colleen A., 1967- author.
Title: Nevada / by Colleen Sexton.
Description: Minneapolis, MN : Bellwether Media, Inc., 2022. |
Series: Blastoff! Discovery: State profiles | Includes bibliographical
    references and index. | Audience: Ages 7-13 | Audience: Grades
    4-6 | Summary: "Engaging images accompany information about
    Nevada. The combination of high-interest subject matter and
    narrative text is intended for students in grades 3 through 8"–
    Provided by publisher.
Identifiers: LCCN 2021020870 (print) | LCCN 2021020871 (ebook)
    | ISBN 9781644873335 (library binding) | ISBN
    9781648341762 (ebook)
Subjects: LCSH: Nevada–Juvenile literature.
Classification: LCC F841.3 .S48 2022 (print) | LCC F841.3 (ebook)
    | DDC 979.3–dc23
LC record available at https://lccn.loc.gov/2021020870
LC ebook record available at https://lccn.loc.gov/2021020871

Editor: Rebecca Sabelko   Designer: Brittany McIntosh

Printed in the United States of America, North Mankato, MN.

TABLE OF CONTENTS

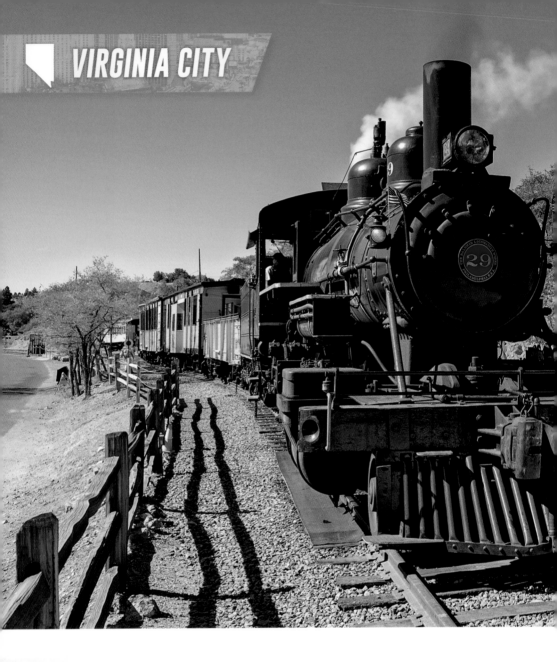

All aboard! A family hops on a train in Virginia City. It rumbles past mining sites in the Comstock hills. Miners struck gold and silver in these hills in the mid-1800s. The family follows a guide deep into the Chollar Mine. They learn about equipment the miners used.

THE COMSTOCK LODE

The Comstock Lode was a silver and gold deposit discovered in 1859. It was worth more than $300 million. Today, that would be several billion dollars!

GREAT BASIN NATIONAL PARK

HOOVER DAM

LAS VEGAS STRIP

VALLEY OF FIRE STATE PARK

The family heads back to town. They stroll down wooden sidewalks. Hotels, an opera house, and mansions line the streets. The family's last stop is an outdoor theater for a Wild West comedy show. Gunslingers and outlaws draw big laughs with their stories and stunts. Welcome to Nevada!

Nevada is in the southwestern United States. Oregon and Idaho lie to the north. Utah and Arizona are Nevada's neighbors to the east. Nevada shares a long border with California to the southwest and west. Carson City is the capital. It sits in west-central Nevada near Lake Tahoe. Other major cities include Las Vegas, Reno, and Henderson.

Nevada covers an area of 110,572 square miles (286,380 square kilometers). Most of the state lies within the **Great Basin**. This region stretches between the Sierra Nevada range to the west and the Rocky Mountains to the east.

CALIFORNIA

N
W+E
S

OREGON

IDAHO

NEVADA

RENO

CARSON CITY

UTAH

LAKE
TAHOE

LAS VEGAS

HENDERSON

ARIZONA

HIDDEN CAVE

Early Native Americans stored items for safekeeping in Hidden Cave in western Nevada. Scientists found spears, tools, fishing gear, and baskets that were about 3,500 years old!

STONE ART OUTSIDE HIDDEN CAVE

Hunters followed bison herds into Nevada thousands of years ago. Over time, Native American groups formed. The Washoe fished along Lake Tahoe. The Shoshone hunted in eastern Nevada. The Northern Paiute lived around Pyramid Lake. The Southern Paiute grew crops in the south.

Fur trappers established trails through Nevada to transport goods in the early 1800s. Mexico claimed Nevada in 1821. The United States won the land in 1848. Early **settlers** set up trading posts where gold-seekers stopped on their way to California. Nevada's population grew quickly after the Comstock Lode was discovered in 1859. Nevada became the 36th state in 1864.

NATIVE PEOPLES OF NEVADA

NORTHERN PAIUTE

- Original lands in western Nevada, east-central California, and eastern Oregon
- Also called Numu

SOUTHERN PAIUTE

- Original lands in southern Nevada, southern Utah, northwestern Arizona, and southeastern California
- Also called Nuwu

WASHOE TRIBE OF NEVADA AND CALIFORNIA

- Original lands along the Sierra Nevada near Lake Tahoe
- Also called Washo, Wa She Shu, and Wašiw

WESTERN SHOSHONE

- Original lands in northeastern Nevada
- Also called Newe

The Great Basin covers most of Nevada. Its grassy valleys and sandy deserts lie between rugged mountain ranges. The Humboldt River flows through the basin. In the northeast, steep ridges flatten into **prairies**. The Mojave Desert covers the state's southern tip. Lake Tahoe sits where the Sierra Nevada range reaches into western Nevada.

LAKE TAHOE

HUMBOLDT RIVER

N
W—E
S

■ MOJAVE DESERT

MOJAVE DESERT

NEVADA'S CHALLENGE: SAVING WATER

Nevada often experiences droughts. Its water supply is limited. Local governments make rules for water usage. Residents try to save water by growing native plants instead of lawns. They also install appliances that use less water.

LAKE TAHOE

SPRING
HIGH: 65°F (18°C)
LOW: 36°F (2°C)

SUMMER
HIGH: 90°F (32°C)
LOW: 53°F (12°C)

FALL
HIGH: 68°F (20°C)
LOW: 36°F (2°C)

WINTER
HIGH: 47°F (8°C)
LOW: 22°F (-6°C)

°F = degrees Fahrenheit
°C = degrees Celsius

Most of Nevada has hot summers and mild winters. Winters are colder in the northeast. Nevada is the driest state in the country. Around 9 inches (23 centimeters) of rain and snow fall each year.

Nevada is home to a variety of animals. Deserts shelter rattlesnakes and desert tortoises. Desert bighorn sheep climb rocky mountainsides. Pronghorn nibble on grasses in the valleys. Sage grouse peck the ground for seeds. In thick forests, mountain lions stalk elk. Herds of wild horses roam many parts of the state.

Bald eagles nest in tall trees along riverbanks. Black bears grab trout from the rushing waters. Great blue herons wade in shallow waters. They wait for small frogs to swim by. White pelicans scoop up small fish as they glide across lakes.

SIDEWINDER RATTLESNAKE

DESERT TORTOISE

SAGE GROUSE

MOUNTAIN LION

GREAT BLUE HERON

DESERT BIGHORN SHEEP

Life Span: up to 15 years
Status: least concern

desert bighorn sheep range =

LEAST CONCERN	NEAR THREATENED	VULNERABLE	ENDANGERED	CRITICALLY ENDANGERED	EXTINCT IN THE WILD	EXTINCT

About 3 million people live in Nevada. Most residents crowd into Las Vegas, Reno, and Carson City. About three of every four Nevadans live in the Las Vegas area. More than half of the state's population was not born in Nevada. Many newcomers moved there from other states. Others arrived from Mexico, the Philippines, and El Salvador.

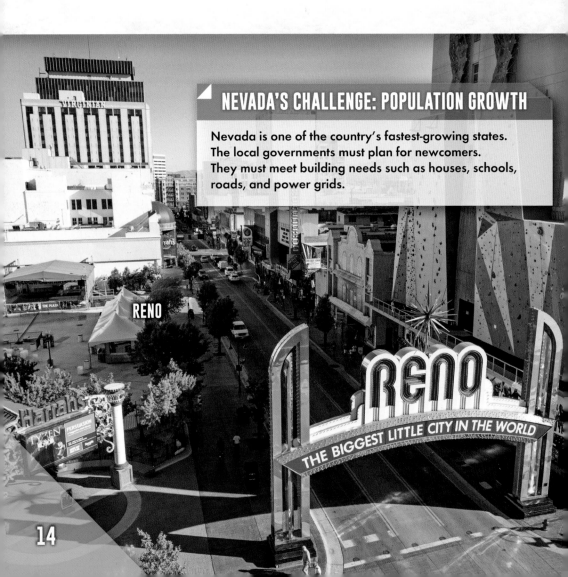

RENO

NEVADA'S CHALLENGE: POPULATION GROWTH

Nevada is one of the country's fastest-growing states. The local governments must plan for newcomers. They must meet building needs such as houses, schools, roads, and power grids.

RENO
THE BIGGEST LITTLE CITY IN THE WORLD

FAMOUS NEVADAN

Name: Andre Agassi
Born: April 29, 1970
Hometown: Las Vegas, Nevada
Famous For: A tennis star who won eight Grand Slam titles between 1992 and 2003 and created the Andre Agassi Foundation for Education

Most Nevadans have **ancestors** from Europe. Some were **Basque** people from the border region of France and Spain. More than one in four Nevadans is Hispanic. Small numbers of Black or African Americans, Native Americans, and Asian Americans call the state home.

BASQUE DANCERS

Carson City began as a stopover for travelers during the California **Gold Rush**. But its population boomed after the Comstock Lode gold and silver discoveries. Carson City was named the capital when Nevada became a state in 1864.

KIT CARSON

Carson City is named for the famous frontiersman Christopher "Kit" Carson. He was a fur trapper, explorer, guide, and soldier. He also helped map northern Nevada.

16

Today, museums and historic buildings help preserve Carson City's history. The city's **cultural** center is the Brewery Arts Center. It offers theater performances, concerts, and art classes. Residents shop in the historic downtown district. They also enjoy trails in the city's many parks. Nearby mountains and **canyons** offer places for hiking, river rafting, and skiing.

INDUSTRY

NEW YORK-NEW YORK
HOTEL AND CASINO
LAS VEGAS

VALET/SELF
HOTEL LOBB
Mlife PLAYE
RESTROOMS

Tourism is a big business in Nevada. More than 50 million people visit the state each year. Around four out of five workers have **service jobs**. Many Nevadans serve tourists in casinos, hotels, and restaurants in Las Vegas and Reno.

Gold is Nevada's most important mineral. Miners also dig up copper and silver. Few crops grow in Nevada's poor soil. Ranchers plant alfalfa and hay to feed large herds of cattle and sheep. Factories make products from metals, plastics, and rubber. The U.S. military employs thousands of workers at Nellis Air Force Base and other national defense sites.

INVENTED IN NEVADA

ZIPNUT
Date Invented: 1983
Inventor: Robert Fullerton

ALL-YOU-CAN-EAT BUFFET
Date Invented: 1956
Inventor: Herbert Cobb McDonald

RIVETED JEANS
Date Invented: 1871
Inventor: Jacob Davis

FOOD

ALL-YOU-CAN-EAT
BUFFET

Nevada's restaurants offer **cuisines** from around the world. Thai dishes and sushi are specialties. Las Vegas's casinos introduced all-you-can-eat buffets in the 1950s. Guests eat as much as they want for a low price. Nevada's cattle ranches make beef popular. Cooks serve up steaks, hamburgers, and stews.

20

Basque meals are a favorite in northern Nevada. *Paella* is a flavorful Spanish-style dish. Nevadans also enjoy **traditional** pasties that workers once carried into mines. These handheld pies feature meat and potatoes in a flaky pastry. Some popular desserts date to the 1800s. They include potato-caramel cake and saffron cake.

PAELLA

POTATO-CARAMEL CAKE

SHEEPHERDER CHILI

16 SERVINGS

Have an adult help you make this hearty dish!

INGREDIENTS

3 pounds ground beef

4 tablespoons dried onions

1/4 cup chili powder

1 tablespoon cumin

2 tablespoons Worcestershire sauce

1 teaspoon garlic powder

1/4 teaspoon cayenne pepper

1 teaspoon oregano

1 teaspoon vinegar

1 can stewed tomatoes

1 can tomato sauce

salt to taste

black pepper to taste

water as necessary

DIRECTIONS

1. Brown the ground beef in a heavy pot. Drain off the fat.

2. Add the other ingredients.

3. Simmer for at least 2 hours, adding water as needed.

4. Thicken with flour, if desired. Serve over rice and enjoy!

Nevada offers many outdoor adventures. Hikers and rock climbers head to the state's many parks. Lake Tahoe, Lake Mead, and Pyramid Lake are great places for swimming and waterskiing. Snowboarders hit the state's snowy slopes. Fishers catch bass, trout, and salmon in Nevada's rivers.

HOOVER DAM

The Hoover Dam spans the Colorado River between Nevada and Arizona. Around 7 million people tour the dam each year. This enormous concrete structure is 726 feet (221 meters) tall. It provides electricity to about 1.3 million people.

Las Vegas is famous for fun and entertainment. The bright lights of the Las Vegas Strip draw crowds from around the world. Visitors and locals enjoy stage shows, casinos, and restaurants. The city also hosts men's professional hockey, soccer, and football teams. Fans also cheer for the Las Vegas Aces women's professional basketball team.

LAS VEGAS

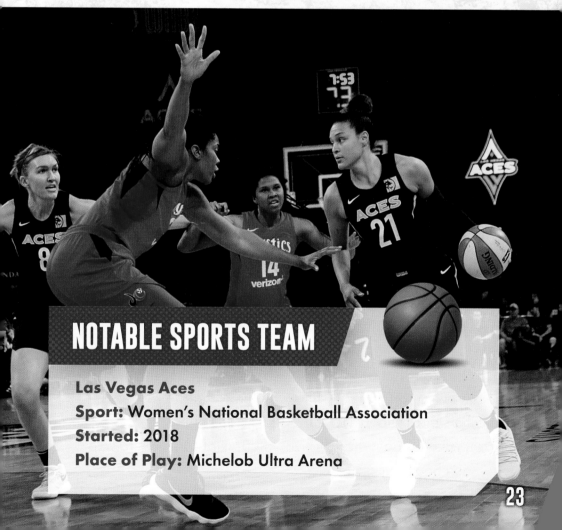

NOTABLE SPORTS TEAM

Las Vegas Aces
Sport: Women's National Basketball Association
Started: 2018
Place of Play: Michelob Ultra Arena

SILVER STATE STAMPEDE

Nevadans honor their Western roots at rodeos across the state every summer. The Silver State Stampede in Elko is Nevada's oldest rodeo. Elko also hosts the National Basque Festival every July. This festival features bread-making and wood-chopping contests.

Nevada Day in Carson City salutes the day Nevada became a state. Every October, crowds line the streets for a huge parade that celebrates Nevada's community spirit. The Pahrump Social **Powwow** celebrates Native American cultures each November. It includes drummers, dancers, and artists from many Western tribes. Nevadans come together to celebrate their rich **heritage**!

UP TO SPEED

The Reno Air Races thrill huge crowds every September. Pilots race planes around a course at speeds of up to 500 miles (805 kilometers) per hour!

1859

The Comstock Lode, a reserve of gold and silver, is discovered in western Nevada

1776

Francisco Garcés of Spain may have been the first European to reach Nevada

1840s

Kit Carson explores and helps map northern Nevada

1848

The United States takes control of Nevada after the Mexican-American War

1821

Mexico takes control of Nevada from Spain

1864

Nevada becomes the 36th state

1936

Construction of the Hoover Dam is completed

2002

The U.S. government chooses Nevada's Yucca Mountain as the main storage site for the nation's nuclear waste

1931

Governor Fred Balzar signs a law that makes casino gambling legal in Nevada

2018

Nevada becomes the first state to elect a majority of women in its state legislature

1986

Nevada's first national park, Great Basin National Park, opens

NEVADA FACTS

Nickname: The Silver State

Motto: All for Our Country

Date of Statehood: October 31, 1864 (the 36th state)

Capital City: Carson City ★

Other Major Cities: Las Vegas, Henderson, Reno

Area: 110,572 square miles (286,380 square kilometers); Nevada is the 7th largest state.

Population

3,104,614
(2020)

STATE FLAG

Nevada's state flag has a blue background. A banner with the words *Battle Born* hangs in the upper left corner. It refers to Nevada joining the Union during the Civil War. The state name and a silver star sit under the banner. The star stands for Nevada's state metal, silver. Two branches of sagebrush, the state flower, curve up on either side to meet the banner.

INDUSTRY

Main Exports

gold

copper

electronics

chemicals

JOBS

MANUFACTURING
3%

FARMING AND NATURAL RESOURCES
1%

GOVERNMENT
10%

SERVICES
86%

Natural Resources
tungsten, gold, silver, copper, oil, sand and gravel

GOVERNMENT

Federal Government
4 REPRESENTATIVES | **2** SENATORS

6 ELECTORAL VOTES

NV

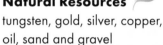
USA

State Government
42 REPRESENTATIVES | **21** SENATORS

STATE SYMBOLS

STATE BIRD
MOUNTAIN BLUEBIRD

STATE ANIMAL
DESERT BIGHORN SHEEP

STATE FLOWER
SAGEBRUSH

STATE INSECT
VIVID DANCER DAMSELFLY

ancestors—relatives who lived long ago

Basque—referring to people who live in the western Pyrenees Mountains between France and Spain

canyons—deep and narrow valleys that have steep sides

cuisines—styles of cooking

cultural—related to the beliefs, arts, and ways of life in a place or society

gold rush—the rapid movement of Americans to the western part of the country after gold was discovered in the mid-1800s

Great Basin—a broad, dry region in the western United States that does not drain to an ocean; the Great Basin spreads across parts of Utah, Nevada, Oregon, Idaho, and California.

heritage—the traditions, achievements, and beliefs that are part of the history of a group of people

powwow—a Native American gathering that usually includes dancing

prairies—large, open areas of grassland

service jobs—jobs that perform tasks for people or businesses

settlers—people who move to live in a new, undeveloped region

tourism—the business of people traveling to visit other places

traditional—related to customs, ideas, or beliefs handed down from one generation to the next

TO LEARN MORE

AT THE LIBRARY

Baptiste, Tracey. *If You Were a Kid in the Wild West.* New York, N.Y.: Children's Press, 2018.

Gregory, Josh. *Nevada*. New York, N.Y.: Children's Press, 2018.

Stefoff, Rebecca. *Building the Hoover Dam*. New York, N.Y.: Cavendish Square Publishing, 2018.

ON THE WEB

FACTSURFER

Factsurfer.com gives you a safe, fun way to find more information.

1. Go to www.factsurfer.com.

2. Enter "Nevada" into the search box and click 🔍.

3. Select your book cover to see a list of related content.

INDEX